Introduction

A journey toward inner awakening

We live in a world full of wonders. Yet despite its wonders, it is often filled with stress, conflicts, and constant distractions. In the search for meaning and balance, we often struggle with our own emotional wounds, spiritual blockages, and daily challenges that seem to pull us away from our true essence. However, there is a bright path toward healing, inner peace, and personal fulfillment. A journey that begins with the exploration and opening of your inner world. This guide is designed to accompany you on this transformative adventure, offering you the tools needed to reconnect with yourself and unlock your hidden potential.

Imagine a space where pain and wounds are not insurmountable obstacles, but opportunities for growth and healing. Imagine an existence where each mindful breath releases accumulated tensions, where each directed intention transforms your inner reality, and where mindfulness becomes a faithful companion in your quest for serenity. This is what we invite you to discover through this work. You will learn to embrace pain in order to better understand it, cultivate mindfulness to reconnect with your essence, and use conscious breathing to release emotional blockages.

The journey you are about to embark on is also one of forgiveness and release from the past. Learn the art of forgiveness, not only towards others but also towards yourself, to break free from the chains of the past and embrace a future filled with possibilities.

Discover the power of affirmations and intentions to reprogram your mind, heal your emotions, and transform your inner reality. You will also dive into reconnecting with your inner child, an essential process for restoring harmony and the joy of living, often lost in the turbulence of adulthood.

As you progress through the chapters, you will be guided to balance your chakras and harmonize your emotional body. Each energy center, from the root chakra to the crown chakra, plays a crucial role in your well-being. You will learn how to open and balance these chakras, allowing your vital energy to flow freely, bringing you peace and vitality.

We will also discuss gratitude and self-love as powerful tools to soothe wounds and strengthen your sense of wholeness. Letting go and spiritual resilience will be central to your exploration as well. Learn the art of detachment to navigate emotional challenges with wisdom and flexibility. Discover practices to cultivate resilience and rise above difficulties with renewed inner strength. Finally, we invite you to create a sacred space—both physical and mental—to nourish your soul. Design a space that inspires you and supports your spiritual journey, and integrate regular practices to maintain this sacred space as a constant refuge for your well-being.

This guide is more than a series of techniques; it is an invitation to a profound and personal journey toward a more fulfilled and harmonious life. It's about discovering how, through spiritual liberation and the opening of your inner chakras, you can transform not only your inner life but also your experience of the world. Each chapter is designed to provide you with practical tools, concrete exercises, and clear guidance to help you unlock your potential and live a life full of meaning and serenity.

We encourage you to approach each page with curiosity and openness, allowing these practices to resonate deeply within you. May this journey toward inner awakening bring you newfound clarity, lasting peace, and an authentic connection with your purest essence. Welcome to this transformative journey, where each step brings you closer to the wholeness and well-being you deserve.

Chapter I
Embrace the pain to better understand it

Emotional pain is a universal experience, as human as breathing. Yet, in our modern culture, we often do everything in our power to avoid it. We run from it, drown it out with distractions, or hide it behind forced smiles. However, avoiding emotional pain only makes things worse in the long run. Embracing pain is an essential step toward healing and understanding what it has to teach us. This chapter explores why it is so important to confront our pain, how to welcome it with compassion, and which spiritual methods can help us transform this suffering into a source of deep healing.

Pain as a Messenger

The first thing to understand is that emotional pain is not your enemy. In reality, it is a subtle form of communication from your body and mind. It signals that a part of you is hurt, neglected, or out of balance. Just as physical pain indicates that we need to heal a bodily wound, emotional pain shows us where attention, love, and healing are needed on a psychological and spiritual level.

Ignoring or suppressing pain can lead to harmful long-term effects, such as anxiety disorders, depression, or destructive behaviors. However, when we choose to listen to and embrace it, we can begin to understand its source and deeper causes. Pain then becomes an opportunity for personal and spiritual transformation.

Facing Pain: A Difficult First Step

Facing pain is one of the most challenging steps in any healing process. Our natural instinct is to avoid what hurts, but the irony is that the more we avoid pain, the stronger it becomes in silence. It takes root deep within our subconscious, where it can manifest as repressed anger, resentment, apathy, or self-sabotaging behaviors.

Facing pain means acknowledging that it exists. It involves giving yourself permission to feel everything you feel, without judgment or shame.

Embracing pain means coming into contact with your emotions without trying to run from or manipulate them. It's not an easy task and requires a certain degree of courage and vulnerability. But it is also one of the most liberating steps toward healing.

The Practice of Mindful Presence

One of the most powerful methods for embracing pain is the practice of mindfulness, or mindful presence. Mindfulness involves observing your thoughts, emotions, and physical sensations with attention, without trying to change or judge them. It helps ground you in the present moment and connect to what you're truly feeling, instead of getting lost in past or future scenarios.

Imagine yourself sitting in silence, eyes closed, ready to observe what's happening within you. You can start by focusing on your breath, noticing how the air moves in and out of your lungs. Then, gently turn your attention to your body. Where do you feel tension, discomfort, or pain? Take the time to explore these sensations without judgment.

Next, observe your emotions. Is there sadness, fear, anger, or another emotion arising? Instead of fleeing from these emotions, allow them to be present. Say to yourself internally, "I feel this pain, and that's okay. I'm no longer running from it; I'm embracing it." By practicing this mindful presence, you learn to be with your emotions rather than fighting against them. This can create an inner space where healing can begin.

The Importance of Self-Compassion

Welcoming pain with compassion is a key element of the healing process. Often, when we feel emotional pain, we tend to be very hard on ourselves. We judge ourselves for being vulnerable or blame ourselves for our emotions. This type of self-criticism only intensifies the suffering.

Self-compassion involves treating our emotions with the same kindness and understanding that we would offer a close friend. Instead of judging yourself for what you feel, you can say, "It's okay to feel this. I'm going through a tough time, and I deserve to be treated with gentleness." This doesn't mean wallowing in your pain, but rather allowing yourself to feel without self-judgment.

A simple exercise in self-compassion is to place your hand on your heart when you feel emotional pain, and say soothing words to yourself. For example, you might say, "This is a moment of suffering. I give myself permission to feel this pain. I'm here for myself, with love and compassion."

Pain as an Opportunity for Growth

Embracing pain doesn't mean passively enduring it. It can also be an opportunity to grow and learn about yourself. Emotional pain often has deep roots, stemming from childhood wounds, limiting beliefs, or past traumas. By fully embracing it, you begin to uncover these underlying layers of your psyche.

Once you can see the pain clearly, you can start asking important questions: What is this pain trying to tell me? What part of myself needs healing? Are there beliefs I still hold that no longer serve me? This kind of introspection can open the door to deep transformation, allowing you to release old wounds and rebuild your life on healthier foundations.

Spiritual Practices for Embracing Pain

Certain spiritual practices can be especially beneficial in welcoming emotional pain and facilitating healing. One of these is heart-centered meditation. This meditation involves focusing on your heart center and breathing deeply, while imagining that each breath brings love and light to your wounded heart.

It's a way to nourish your inner being with compassion and healing. Another spiritual practice is the ritual of letting go. For example, you can write a letter to yourself or to someone else, and then dispose of it by tearing it up or burning it, symbolizing the release of what no longer serves you.

This approach can greatly help transform and release blocked emotional energy. You can also visualize pain as a cloud or a shadow. After a deep breath, exhale and imagine this shadow leaving your body and drifting far away until it's no longer recognizable. This symbol can aid in releasing your suffering. Then, engage in prayer or mantras. By repeating positive affirmations or sacred mantras with closed eyes, you can soothe your mind and bring a sense of inner peace.

Welcoming emotional pain in order to heal it is an act of courage and self-love. It means you no longer want to dwell in suffering, but rather accept it as a natural part of the human experience, while taking steps to heal it.

By opening your heart to your own suffering, you create space for healing, understanding, and spiritual transformation. Far from being a weakness, this process of welcoming is a demonstration of your inner strength and commitment to your emotional well-being. It is the first step that will guide you toward a more balanced, authentic, and fulfilling life.

Chapter II
Cultivating Mindfulness to Reconnect with Yourself

In our modern world, where everything seems to move at a dizzying pace, it's easy to get lost in the noise of thoughts, responsibilities, and external distractions. We often spend our days on "autopilot," not paying attention to what's actually happening within us. However, mindfulness, or the art of being fully present in the moment, is a crucial key to reconnecting with yourself and finding inner peace. This chapter will explain how to cultivate mindfulness to better understand your inner world, with concrete examples, practical tips, and simple ideas for integrating this practice into your daily life.

Understanding Mindfulness

Mindfulness is defined as a spiritual state in which you bring conscious, non-judgmental attention to the present moment. In other words, it means observing your thoughts, emotions, and physical sensations without trying to change or push them away. Mindfulness helps you connect with your body and mind, promoting greater self-awareness. This practice is especially powerful for reducing stress, calming anxiety, and fostering greater mental clarity.

The concept of mindfulness has its roots in ancient spiritual traditions, notably Buddhism, but has been embraced by modern psychology and validated by scientific studies for its benefits on mental and emotional health. Today, many people use mindfulness not only to calm themselves but also to reconnect with their deep self, uncovering forgotten or ignored facets of themselves.

Reconnecting with yourself means being in harmony with your emotions, thoughts, desires, and needs. When you disconnect from your inner self, you risk becoming reactive to external situations, feeling empty or lost, and losing sight of what is truly important to you. Conversely, when you are connected to yourself, you can make more conscious choices, live in harmony with your values, and experience a greater sense of balance and peace.

A simple way to start cultivating mindfulness is to pay attention to your breath. Breath is a powerful anchor that brings you back to the present moment, as it is always there, accessible at any time.

To practice breathing effectively, find a quiet place where you can sit or lie down comfortably.

Close your eyes and begin to focus on your natural breath. There is no need to alter your breathing; just observe it.

Notice the sensation of the air entering and leaving your nostrils, your lungs, and focus on the rise and fall of your chest or abdomen.

Whenever your mind wanders into thoughts or distractions, gently bring it back to your breath, without judgment. To help maintain this focus on yourself, you can count each breath up to ten, then start over. For example, inhale and count "one," exhale and count "two," and so on up to ten. This will help anchor your mind as you begin. This simple exercise can be practiced for a few minutes each day and is particularly effective for calming a restless mind and reconnecting with your body.

Once you have mastered this initial exercise, you can extend it to the rest of your body. Experiencing your whole body is another mindfulness practice that helps you reconnect fully with it and your physical sensations. This exercise is especially useful for detecting tension, emotional blocks, or stress areas in the body. To do this, lie on your back in a calm and comfortable place.

Keep your eyes closed and start by taking a few deep breaths to relax. Focus on your feet and become aware of all the sensations present in this area. Is there warmth, cold, tension, or a sense of lightness? Slowly move your attention through each part of your body: your ankles, calves, knees, thighs, abdomen, chest, shoulders, arms, hands, neck, and finally, your head.

At each stage, simply observe the sensations without trying to change them. If you notice any tension, you can visualize the area relaxing with each exhale. This body scan will help not only release physical tension but also gain insight into where some of your unresolved emotions might be stored.

However, mindfulness is not limited to formal meditation sessions. You can also integrate it into your daily activities to reconnect with yourself throughout the day.

For example, you might eat a meal or snack mindfully. Eat slowly, savor each bite, and notice all the flavors, textures, and sensations in your mouth. Put down your utensils between bites, breathe, and be attentive to your experience.

You can also continue mindfulness exercises in your environment while on the move. When you walk, instead of losing yourself in thoughts, focus on the sensations of your feet touching the ground, the movements of your body, and the sounds and smells around you. Walking mindfully is a soothing way to reconnect with the present moment.

Finally, apply mindfulness to household tasks. Choose a daily task you generally find mundane, such as washing dishes or folding laundry, and practice it mindfully. Be present with each movement, each tactile sensation, and notice your internal state. This transforms simple tasks into moments of active meditation.

Mindfulness does not require hours of daily meditation. Start with a few minutes each day and gradually increase the duration if you wish. Even a brief and regular practice can have powerful effects.

In the beginning, be gentle with yourself: Mindfulness is not about perfection. It's normal for your mind to wander or for you to feel frustrated. The key is to gently bring your attention back to the present moment, without judgment. To help refocus your mind, place visual reminders in your environment, such as a note on your desk or an alarm on your phone, to remind you to take mindful breaks throughout the day.

Also, create conscious transition moments and use them in your day to practice mindfulness.

For example, when transitioning from one task to another or moving from one room to another, take a mindful breath and return to the present moment. If you have difficulty meditating alone, consider using guided meditations available through apps or online videos. They can help you stay focused and develop your practice.

Mindfulness for Calming Emotions

Mindfulness is also a powerful tool for managing and soothing difficult emotions. When you experience anger, sadness, anxiety, or stress, your first reaction is often to push them away. However, by practicing mindfulness, you learn to welcome these emotions with gentleness and curiosity, without judgment.

For example, if you feel anxiety, instead of focusing on thoughts that amplify the emotion, you can ground yourself in your breath and simply observe how anxiety manifests in your body. Perhaps you feel tension in your stomach or an increased heart rate. Instead of fleeing from these sensations, allow yourself to observe and accept them as part of your experience. This simple acknowledgment can often reduce the intensity of the emotions.

Cultivating mindfulness is a path to greater connection with yourself and allows you to reconnect with your inner self. By taking the time to be present with your thoughts, emotions, and body, you open the door to greater inner peace and a better understanding of yourself. Mindfulness is a simple yet powerful practice that can transform your relationship with yourself and, by extension, the world around you. In daily life, it's easy to get lost in external chaos, but by returning to the present moment, you give yourself the opportunity to find your center, listen to your inner self, and cultivate a profound sense of well-being.

Chapter III
Releasing Emotional Blockages with Conscious Breathing

Breathing is one of the most powerful tools for releasing emotional blockages and restoring inner balance. Often, when we go through intense emotional experiences, we unconsciously hold our breath or adopt shallow breathing patterns, which can create tension in our bodies and block emotional energy. Conscious breathing is a simple yet incredibly effective practice that can help you untangle these tensions, release blocked energies, and facilitate emotional healing.

In this chapter, you will explore various conscious breathing techniques that promote emotional and energetic release. You will also learn how to recognize signs of healing and transformation while integrating these practices into your daily routine.

The Importance of Breathing for Emotional Healing

Breathing plays a central role in our physical, emotional, and energetic well-being. As a direct link between the body and mind, it can affect your emotional and mental states. When you breathe deeply and consciously, you allow your body to release tension and let energy flow more freely.

Unresolved emotions, such as fear, anger, or sadness, can be stored in the body as muscular tension or energetic blockages. These blockages can lead to physical pain, fatigue, or a general sense of emotional exhaustion. Practicing conscious breathing helps release these tensions and promotes energy flow in the body, allowing these emotions to be acknowledged, felt, and eventually released.

One of the simplest and most effective techniques for releasing emotional blockages is diaphragmatic breathing. This type of breathing, also known as abdominal or deep breathing, engages the diaphragm, a muscle located under the lungs, and allows for a more complete and soothing breath.

To practice this breathing technique, sit or lie comfortably on your back. Place one hand on your chest and the other on your abdomen.

Close your eyes and begin to breathe in slowly through your nose.

Feel your abdomen rise under your hand as you inhale, while your chest remains relatively still. Exhale slowly through your mouth, and feel your abdomen fall. Repeat this exercise for 5 to 10 minutes, maintaining a slow, deep, and steady breath.

Diaphragmatic breathing stimulates the parasympathetic nervous system, which is responsible for relaxation and bodily recovery. By fostering a state of calm and relaxation, this technique helps release accumulated physical and emotional tension. It also brings the body back to a state of stability, reducing feelings of stress and anxiety.

Another breathing technique is alternate nostril breathing, or "Nadi Shodhana" in Sanskrit. This yogic technique is designed to balance the two hemispheres of the brain and soothe emotional fluctuations. It is particularly beneficial for individuals who feel emotionally overwhelmed or have difficulty stabilizing their thoughts and feelings.

To make the most of this breathing technique, sit comfortably with your spine straight and your eyes closed. Using your right hand, place your thumb on your right nostril to close it, and inhale slowly through your left nostril. At the end of the inhale, close your left nostril with your ring finger and exhale slowly through your right nostril. Now inhale through your right nostril, close it, and exhale through your left nostril. Continue this cycle for 5 to 10 minutes, alternating nostrils with each breath.

This technique balances energies in the body and calms the mind by soothing excessive thoughts. Alternate nostril breathing helps regulate the flow of energy through the energetic channels called "nadis" in yogic tradition. When these channels are harmonized, you may experience greater emotional and mental clarity.

If you seek to access altered states of consciousness that facilitate emotional healing and personal transformation, holotropic breathing is a powerful method that can help you reach this level of fullness. Developed by psychiatrist Stanislav Grof, this technique involves rapid, deep breaths that allow for a cathartic release of emotional blockages.

Warning: This practice can be intense, and it is advisable to explore it under the supervision of a therapist or experienced guide, especially if you have a history of significant trauma or mental health issues.

To practice this technique effectively, place yourself in a safe and comfortable space where you won't be disturbed. Lie on your back and close your eyes. Begin to breathe deeply and rapidly, inhaling and exhaling through your mouth without pauses between breaths. Let your body find a natural rhythm while maintaining a rapid and continuous breath. Allow your emotions to surface without judgment or restraint.

Continue this practice for 20 to 30 minutes, or longer if you feel comfortable. The goal is to let the breath guide the release process. Holotropic breathing allows you to release deeply buried emotions by creating a state of expanded consciousness. This state can facilitate access to unresolved emotional experiences, often linked to past traumas or unconscious patterns. By traversing these emotions, the body and mind can release them, leading to a sense of clarity and lightness.

However, conscious breathing can also be practiced in movement, which can be particularly useful for releasing energetic blockages that manifest physically. For example, combining breathing with gentle movements such as yoga, tai chi, or intuitive dance can help unlock deeply rooted tensions in the body.

To practice conscious breathing in movement, start by standing in a safe place and taking a few deep breaths. Then, allow your body to move spontaneously in rhythm with your breath. You might stretch, shake your arms, or perform circular movements with your hips. Each movement should be guided by your breath. Inhale while raising your arms or opening your chest, and exhale while relaxing or bending forward. The goal is to release blocked energy by allowing your body to express itself freely, without judgment.

Combining conscious movement with breathing helps release physical and emotional tensions while restoring energy flow in the body. This facilitates a cathartic release and strengthens the connection between body and mind, which can help restore a general sense of well-being.

Conscious breathing practices are subtle yet powerful tools for freeing yourself from emotional and energetic blockages. Here are some signs that these practices are working for you: After practicing conscious breathing, you should experience inner calm, reduced stress and anxiety, and greater mental clarity. You might feel waves of emotion during or after the practice, such as tears, laughter, or even anger. These emotions are signs that the body is releasing tension and emotional blockages. Welcome them without judgment.

After releasing emotional blockages, you might feel a sense of lightness, as if a weight has been lifted from your shoulders. Your energy may flow more freely, and you might feel more alive and aligned. You may begin to notice changes in your thoughts and behaviors, becoming more aware of your emotions, mental patterns, and reactions to emotional situations.

Physical tensions related to emotional blockages may also begin to disappear, with improvements in posture, reduced muscle pain, and better digestion.

Conscious breathing is a powerful tool. By integrating simple practices like diaphragmatic breathing, alternate nostril breathing, or deeper methods like holotropic breathing, you can help your body and mind release repressed emotions and regain balance.

These practices require no special equipment and can be incorporated into your daily routine, whether during moments of calm or in movement. With patience and consistency, you will start to observe changes in your emotional, physical, and energetic well-being, bringing you closer to healing and inner harmony.

Chapter IV
Releasing the Past through the Art of Forgiveness

Forgiveness is one of the most profound and transformative spiritual practices. When we choose to forgive, whether ourselves or others, we release the invisible chains that bind us to the past and prevent us from moving towards a freer and more fulfilling life. However, forgiveness is often misunderstood. Many believe that forgiving means forgetting or minimizing the pain caused by past wounds, but in reality, forgiveness is an act of personal liberation. It is a process through which we decide no longer to let past events control our present and future. In this chapter, you will explore the spiritual path of forgiveness and the steps to free yourself from emotional wounds through this powerful practice.

Forgiveness does not mean excusing the hurtful actions of others or forgetting the pain that was felt. It is not about accepting unacceptable behavior or allowing someone to continue hurting you. On the contrary, forgiveness is a conscious choice to release anger, resentment, and pain associated with past events. These negative emotions can act as toxins in your life, blocking your emotional, mental, and spiritual well-being.

By forgiving, you decide to let go of the hold these wounds have on you. You stop reliving the pain and suffering, allowing your mind and heart to heal. Forgiveness also enables you to reclaim your personal power, as long as you remain attached to anger or revenge, you remain mentally and emotionally tied to those who have hurt you.

Nevertheless, forgiveness is not only about others; it is also about the relationship we have with ourselves. We are often our own harshest critics, blaming ourselves for past mistakes, decisions made out of fear or lack of discernment. This guilt or shame can become a heavy burden, preventing love and kindness towards ourselves from entering.

Forgiving oneself means accepting our humanity, recognizing that we make mistakes and that these mistakes do not define our worth. It involves offering oneself the same compassion and kindness that we would offer to a close friend. When you forgive yourself, you stop punishing yourself for the past and open the door to a more aligned and serene life.

The process of forgiveness is unique to each individual, but there are common steps that can guide this inner journey. It is a task that requires time, patience, and self-compassion. Here is a five-step spiritual process to help you release the past through forgiveness.

Acknowledge and Accept the Pain

The first step in forgiveness is to acknowledge and accept the pain caused by past events. This may seem counterintuitive, but it is essential to allow this suffering to be fully felt before you can release it. Too often, we suppress or avoid our negative emotions, hoping they will disappear with time. However, this suppression only prolongs the pain.

Take time to sit with your emotions. Allow yourself to fully feel the sadness, anger, or disappointment resulting from the wounds you have experienced. You can write in a journal, meditate, or simply allow yourself to cry. Recognizing and validating your pain is a crucial step toward healing.

For a practical example: Sit in a quiet place and close your eyes. Breathe deeply and focus on the feelings related to the person or situation you wish to forgive. Try not to judge or reject what you feel; simply let these emotions emerge. It may be helpful to mentally ask yourself: "What am I really feeling?"

Make the Decision to Forgive

Forgiveness begins with a conscious decision. It is not a spontaneous feeling that appears out of nowhere; it is a choice. This choice can be difficult, as it often involves letting go of feelings of anger, resentment, or revenge. However, making this decision is an act of liberation. You choose not to be a prisoner of the past, not to let bitterness dominate your life.

It is important to note that this decision does not mean you must forgive immediately. Sometimes, it takes time for the heart to follow the intention. But by making this decision, you are already engaging in the process.

Repeat inwardly or out loud: "I choose to forgive. I release this pain for my well-being." Do this each day, even if you do not yet feel an immediate change.

Understand and View the Situation from a New Perspective

One of the keys to forgiveness is to cultivate compassion, not only for yourself but also for those who have hurt you. This does not mean excusing their behavior but rather trying to understand their motivations, pain, and human limitations.

Often, those who hurt others act out of their own suffering. By stepping back, putting yourself in their shoes, and viewing the situation from another angle, you can begin to diffuse the emotional intensity linked to the wound. You do not have to agree with what they did, but understanding the source of their behavior can facilitate the forgiveness process.

Subsequently, try to visualize the person who hurt you as a complex human being with their own suffering, fears, and stories. Ask yourself: "What inner wounds might have led this person to act this way?" This reflection can open a space for compassion and letting go.

Release Negative Emotions

Once you have made the decision to forgive and cultivated compassion, it is time to release the negative emotions attached to the event. This can be done through specific practices such as meditation, visualization, or symbolic rituals.

Compassion meditation (or Metta meditation) is particularly powerful for releasing negative emotions. It involves sending thoughts of love and kindness to yourself and then to the other person. This may seem difficult at first, especially if the pain is still fresh, but over time, it helps dissolve resentments.

Sit in a quiet place. Start by sending thoughts of love and kindness to yourself: "May I be at peace, may I be happy, may I be free from suffering."

Then direct these thoughts towards the person who hurt you: "May you be at peace, may you be happy, may you be free from suffering."

This may be uncomfortable at first, but persevere. The goal is not to approve of what they did but to release your heart from negative emotions.

Embrace Complete Letting Go

The final step of forgiveness is complete letting go. This does not mean forgetting what happened, but rather ceasing to let this event dictate your emotions and reactions. You no longer allow this pain to control your life.

Forgiveness then becomes a practice integrated into your daily life. Whenever you feel anger or sadness, return to your intention to forgive and release. This can be an ongoing process, but over time, the weight of the wound lightens until you are completely free.

To better understand how to achieve this state of letting go, here is a highly effective practical exercise. Write a letter to the person who hurt you, explaining what you felt at that moment and expressing your willingness to forgive. However, you do not need to send this letter; the goal is to express and release your emotions. Once the letter is complete, burn it in a symbolic ritual to signify your intention to let go and release the past.

Forgiveness is a gradual process, and it can be difficult to know if you have truly forgiven. Here are some signs that indicate progress in this process:

One sign that you have made progress is when, upon thinking about the person or event, the emotional intensity you feel is diminished. You experience less anger, sadness, or resentment. Additionally, you are no longer attached to the past; you can talk about the event without being upset or falling into an emotional spiral.

By releasing the pain, you experience emotional lightness and an increased sense of freedom.

Forgiveness allows you to welcome more inner peace and feel aligned with your past. You are thus more at peace with yourself.

Forgiveness is an act of love and deep healing. By releasing past wounds, we create space for peace, joy, and spiritual growth in our lives. It is a personal and spiritual process that takes time but offers immense emotional freedom in return. By forgiving, we not only give a gift to others; we also offer ourselves the chance to live a more fulfilled and peaceful life.

Chapter V
The Power of Intention: Transforming Your Inner Reality

Intention is a powerful force that can profoundly transform our inner reality. By using affirmations and intentions, we have the ability to reprogram our minds and heal our emotions. This process involves not only clearly defining what we wish to achieve but also cultivating a deep conviction that these changes are possible. However, the path to inner transformation is not always straightforward. Mental and emotional obstacles can hinder our progress. This chapter explores how to use the power of intention to transform your inner reality, the potential challenges you may face, and the types of emotions you can heal through this practice.

Intention is more than just a thought or a superficial desire; it is a deep and powerful commitment to change. When we set an intention, we direct our mind and energy towards a specific goal, and we begin to align our actions and beliefs with that goal. Intention has the power to influence our reality by altering how we perceive and interact with the world.

To set an effective intention, it is essential to formulate it clearly and precisely. An intention should be positive, in the present tense, and specific enough to guide your actions and mindset. For example, instead of saying "I want to be happy," a more precise intention could be "I choose to embrace joy in every moment of my daily life." This formulation helps focus your energy on what you wish to manifest.

Affirmations are positive statements that we repeat to reinforce constructive beliefs and transform our mindset, and it is crucial to use them to modify our intention. By repeating affirmations, we can reprogram our minds and influence our emotions. They work by reshaping negative thought patterns and fostering a more positive outlook aligned with our intentions.

To create effective affirmations, it is important to be specific. Formulate your affirmations clearly. For example, instead of saying "I am healthy," you might say "My body is strong, healthy, and filled with positive energy." It is important to phrase these affirmations in the present tense, as if they are already true. This helps create a sense of reality and engages your subconscious. For instance, "I am able to handle all situations with calm and confidence." Also, always stay positive. Avoid negative phrasing and focus on what you want to attract rather than what you want to avoid. For example, instead of "I am not stressed," say "I feel relaxed and serene."

To easily and quickly practice positive affirmations, you can repeat affirmations that match your intention every morning in front of a mirror. For instance, if you are working on self-confidence, you might repeat: "I am confident and capable. Every day, I am growing more." Repeat these affirmations with conviction, visualizing and feeling what it would be like to live this reality.

Nevertheless, reprogramming the mind using intentions and affirmations can encounter several obstacles. These challenges may be related to old thought patterns, limiting beliefs, or even unconscious resistance. Here are some common difficulties and strategies to overcome them. First, there is mental resistance; these are all the deeply ingrained negative thought patterns that can resist change. Your subconscious may doubt the effectiveness of affirmations, especially if they contradict your current beliefs. To overcome this difficulty, you need to be patient and persistent. Mental reprogramming takes time. Reinforce your affirmations with concrete evidence. For example, if you affirm "I am worthy of love," start noting examples where you have received or given love. This process helps create tangible evidence that supports your affirmations.

Next, limiting beliefs, often inherited from childhood or past experiences, can thwart your efforts to change. These beliefs may include thoughts like "I don't deserve happiness" or "I am not good enough." To address this easily, identify them by reflecting on your recurring thoughts. Gradually replace them with affirmations that contradict them. For example, if you have a limiting belief like "I don't deserve success," replace it with "I deserve success and I am capable of achieving it."

Also, be rigorous as lasting change requires consistency. Sometimes, we can be enthusiastic at first but lose interest over time. To maintain consistency, create a daily routine to incorporate your affirmations.

Use visual reminders, such as sticky notes with your affirmations, and commit to regular practice. You can also join support groups or online communities to share your experiences and stay motivated.

Emotions play a central role in our well-being and inner balance. By using affirmations and intentions, we can target specific emotions that need healing. Here are some common emotions you can heal through intention and the appropriate affirmations for each situation.

The first emotion you can heal through intention is anger. Anger is a powerful emotion that, if mishandled, can harm our mental and physical health. To heal anger, you need to recognize and release this emotion, then replace it with affirmations that promote inner peace. For example, use this affirmation: "I release all anger and choose to nurture inner peace and understanding. I am calm and serene." When you feel anger, take a moment to breathe deeply and repeat this affirmation. You can also practice relaxation techniques like meditation or walking in nature to help calm your mind.

Another emotion that can create emotional imbalance is sadness. It is often related to losses or disappointments. To heal sadness, it is essential to allow your emotions to manifest, then focus on affirmations that reinforce joy and hope. For example, repeat: "I allow sadness to express itself, and I now choose to welcome joy and optimism into my life. Every day, I find new reasons to be happy." You can also express your sadness through writing or talking with a trusted friend. Then, practice affirmations that foster a sense of renewal and hope. Visualize the positive aspects of your life and focus on the small things that bring you joy.

Fear is also a strong emotion that can paralyze and hinder your personal growth. Healing fear requires recognizing it, understanding its roots, and replacing anxious thoughts with affirmations that reinforce confidence and security. Use this affirmation to relieve fear: "I face my fears with courage and confidence. I am safe and capable of overcoming all challenges."

Whenever you are faced with a situation that evokes fear, practice relaxation techniques to calm your mind. Repeat the affirmation to ground yourself in confidence. You can also create an action plan to approach the situation proactively, which will help reduce your anxiety.

The power of intention and affirmations lies in their ability to transform our inner reality. By setting clear intentions and using positive affirmations, we have the power to reprogram our minds and heal our emotions. This process can be complex and fraught with obstacles, but it is essential to remain committed and patient. Difficulties such as mental resistance or limiting beliefs can be overcome with perseverance and appropriate strategies.

By healing negative emotions such as anger, sadness, and fear, we create space for inner peace, self-confidence, and a more positive outlook on life. Intention is a powerful tool that, when used with awareness and dedication, can guide us towards deep and lasting personal transformation. By integrating these practices into your daily life, you open the door to a more harmonious and fulfilling inner reality.

Chapter VI
Reconnecting with Your Inner Child to Find Harmony

Reconnecting with your inner child is an essential step in healing emotional wounds from childhood and finding inner harmony. The inner child represents the part of ourselves that experienced childhood events, carrying memories, emotions, and beliefs that influence our adult behavior and well-being. By nurturing this inner child, you can release emotional blockages, reintegrate lost aspects of yourself, and cultivate a more balanced and joyful life. This chapter explores techniques for healing childhood wounds and embracing your inner child with love.

First, it's crucial to understand the origins of childhood wounds and the memories they are linked to. Emotional wounds from childhood often stem from experiences that marked our psychological development. These wounds may result from neglect, abuse, rejection, excessive criticism, or any other event that affected our sense of self and our ability to feel safe and loved.

For example, if a child felt abandoned or neglected by their parents or caregivers, they might develop a deep sense of rejection and insecurity that persists into adulthood. Constant criticism or judgment can lead to low self-esteem and the feeling of never being good enough. Abuse, whether physical or emotional, leaves deep scars that may manifest as fear, anger, or difficulty trusting others. Being compared to a sibling or other children can create feelings of inferiority and self-esteem issues.

To heal childhood wounds and reintegrate the inner child with love, it is crucial to use techniques that access the memories, emotions, and beliefs formed during that time of life. Here are some effective approaches:

One effective approach to healing these wounds is inner child therapy. This involves dialoguing with the part of yourself that is still somehow stuck in the past. It often involves guided visualizations or writing exercises to connect with your inner child and offer the compassion and support they need.

To open the dialogue effectively, find a calm and comfortable place to sit or lie down. Close your eyes, breathe deeply to relax, and imagine yourself meeting your inner child in a safe and comforting space. Observe what they look like, how they feel, and listen to what they have to say. Offer them reassuring words, love, and compassion, and let them know you are there for them and ready to help them heal. Spend a few minutes offering the support they need, then thank them for their presence and openness.

However, this exercise can sometimes be challenging, especially if you have never done it before. Another more accessible technique is expressive writing. This powerful method allows you to explore and express emotions related to childhood experiences. Through writing, you can release buried feelings and become aware of thought patterns or limiting beliefs formed during your childhood.

To do this, take a notebook and write a letter to your inner child, addressing them as if you were speaking to a young child, using gentle and comforting language. Express your regrets for the times you couldn't protect or support them, and assure them that you are now there to help. Write about the dreams and hopes you have for them, and encourage them to express their emotions. Read the letter aloud and let yourself feel the emotions that arise.

Following this letter, engage in playful and creative activities. This helps reconnect with the joy and innocence of childhood. These activities can help release emotional tension and rediscover a sense of freedom and pleasure. Engage in an activity you enjoyed as a child, such as drawing, painting, playing a game, or building something, and immerse yourself in the pleasure of the activity without judgment or pressure. This will help you regain a sense of lightness and connection with your inner child. Make time for these activities regularly, even as an adult, to maintain a balance between your emotional needs and daily life.

Finally, meditation is a useful practice for accessing deep levels of consciousness and healing emotional wounds. Specific guided meditations for healing the inner child can help create a space of peace and comfort.

To meditate effectively, find a quiet place and sit comfortably. Close your eyes and focus on your breathing. Visualize a soft, warm light surrounding and enveloping your inner child, imagining this light gently penetrating areas of pain or wounds, bringing healing and soothing. Stay in this visualization for a few minutes, feeling filled with compassion and love for your inner child.

Healing childhood wounds is a gradual process, and signs of healing can vary from person to person. Indicators that you have begun to reintegrate your inner child and heal emotional wounds include a reduction in excessive emotional reactivity to situations that were once triggering, increased self-confidence, and a more positive self-image unaffected by childhood limiting beliefs. You will also find joy and pleasure in simple activities and feel more in harmony with yourself. Additionally, you may notice improvements in your relationships with others, with a better ability to establish authentic connections and express your needs and emotions constructively.

Reconnecting with your inner child is a fundamental step towards finding harmony and emotional well-being. By using techniques such as inner child therapy, expressive writing, creative activities, and meditation, you can heal childhood wounds and reintegrate this precious part of yourself. The healing process may take time and require patience, but the benefits of such a journey are immense.

Reintegrating your inner child with love and compassion helps release emotional blockages, strengthen self-esteem, and rediscover authentic joy. By caring for this inner child, you create a space for healing and growth that nourishes your inner balance and guides you toward a more harmonious and fulfilling life.

Chapter VII
Balancing the Chakras to Harmonize Your Emotional Body

Chakras are energy centers located along the spine that play a crucial role in maintaining our emotional and physical balance. Each chakra is associated with specific aspects of our well-being and emotions. By balancing these energy centers, you can harmonize your emotional body, improve your health, and foster a state of inner peace. This chapter explores the chakras, their connections to emotions, and offers practices to balance them for achieving inner harmony.

Chakras are points of convergence for vital energy (or prana) in the body. There are seven main chakras aligned along the spine, each with specific functions and emotional associations.

Root Chakra (Muladhara)

Located at the base of the spine near the coccyx and associated with the color red, it relates to our sense of security and stability. Its opening helps us feel grounded and safe, providing a solid foundation for personal growth.

Sacral Chakra (Svadhisthana)

Located in the lower abdomen below the navel and identified by the color orange, it is associated with creativity, sensuality, and emotions. A balanced sacral chakra promotes healthy emotional expression and a deep connection with our creativity and pleasure.

Solar Plexus Chakra (Manipura)

This chakra, located at the stomach level and linked with the color yellow, is related to self-confidence and personal power. Balancing this chakra strengthens our self-esteem and our ability to manifest our intentions.

Heart Chakra (Anahata)

Located in the center of the chest and represented by the color green, it is the seat of love and compassion. An open heart allows us to experience deep relationships and cultivate unconditional love for ourselves and others.

Throat Chakra (Vishuddha)

Located in the throat and associated with the color light blue, it is connected to communication and self-expression. Its opening facilitates authentic expression and the ability to listen to others with empathy.

Third Eye Chakra (Ajna)

This chakra, located between the eyebrows in the center of the forehead and expressed by the color indigo, is related to intuition and inner perception.

Balancing this chakra enhances mental clarity, inner vision, and spiritual understanding.

Crown Chakra (Sahasrara)

Located at the top of the head and associated with either violet or white, it is linked to spiritual connection and higher consciousness. An open crown chakra allows us to connect with our divine essence and experience elevated spiritual awareness.

To balance the chakras and harmonize your emotional body, several practices can be used. These techniques aim to release energy blockages, restore balance, and promote overall well-being.

The first method for balancing is meditation and visualization. These are powerful tools for balancing the chakras and involve focusing on each chakra, releasing tension, and harmonizing energy.

Sit comfortably in a quiet place and close your eyes. Take a few deep breaths to relax and try to visualize each chakra as a glowing disk of the associated color (red, orange, yellow, green, light blue, indigo, violet) along your spine. Focus on each chakra, visualizing a bright light and imagining this light spinning and clearing energy blockages.

Continue by repeating positive affirmations for each chakra, such as:

Root Chakra

"I am safe and grounded."

Sacral Chakra

"I embrace my creativity and welcome my emotions."

Solar Plexus Chakra

"I am powerful and confident in myself."

Heart Chakra

"I open my heart to love and compassion."

Throat Chakra

"I express my truth with clarity and honesty."

Third Eye Chakra

"I trust my intuition and inner wisdom."

Crown Chakra

"I am connected to the universe and my spiritual consciousness."

Additionally, physical exercises such as yoga are equally effective for balancing the chakras. Each yoga pose is designed to activate and harmonize specific energy centers.

Here is a list of easy exercises and poses that will help you achieve the best benefits:

Root Chakra: Mountain Pose (Tadasana)

Stand with your feet hip-width apart, arms at your sides. Ground yourself firmly to the earth and visualize a red light at the base of your spine.

Sacral Chakra: Goddess Pose (Utkata Konasana)

Spread your legs and bend your knees while keeping your back straight. Imagine an orange light in the lower abdomen and focus on your creativity and emotions.

Solar Plexus Chakra: Warrior Pose (Virabhadrasana)

Take a large step forward with one leg, bend the front knee, and extend your arms. Visualize a yellow light at the solar plexus and feel self-confidence.

Heart Chakra: Bridge Pose (Setu Bandhasana)

Lie on your back, bend your knees, and lift your pelvis while supporting your lower back with your hands.

Focus on a green light in the center of your chest and open yourself to love and compassion.

Throat Chakra: Plow Pose (Halasana)

Lie on your back, lift your legs towards the sky, and bring them behind your head. Imagine a light blue light at your throat and focus on self-expression.

Third Eye Chakra: Child's Pose (Balasana)

Kneel, sit on your heels, then lean forward and rest your forehead on the ground. Visualize an indigo light in the center of your forehead and open yourself to intuition.

Crown Chakra: Meditation Pose (Sukhasana)

Sit cross-legged, hands resting on your knees. Focus on a violet light at the top of your head and connect with spiritual consciousness.

These yoga poses, combined with sounds such as mantras or healing frequencies, can also help balance the chakras. Vibrational sounds resonate with the energetic frequencies of the chakras and promote harmony.

Here is a list of mantras you can associate with each chakra:

Root Chakra

"LAM"

Sacral Chakra

"VAM"

Solar Plexus Chakra

"RAM"

Heart Chakra

"YAM"

Throat Chakra

"HAM"

Third Eye Chakra

"OM"

Crown Chakra

"AH"

Chant or listen to these mantras while focusing on the corresponding chakra. You can also use Tibetan singing bowls or tuning forks to produce healing frequencies.

Signs of successful chakra balancing can be observed through various changes in your emotional and physical life. Positive effects and chakra balance may include reduced stress and anxiety. Improved stress management and decreased anxiety can indicate balanced chakras. You may also notice better concentration and more informed decisions, which can signal balance in the third eye chakra. These balances can enhance your relationships and give you a better capacity to express love.

Additionally, you may experience increased self-confidence and personal power, which may indicate balance in the solar plexus chakra.

A balanced throat chakra will help you have clearer and more honest communication.

Thus, balancing the chakras is an essential process for harmonizing the emotional body and promoting overall well-being. By understanding the functions and emotional associations of the chakras and using practices such as meditation, yoga, and sound exercises, you can restore energetic balance and cultivate a more harmonious life.

Regularly taking care of and balancing your chakras allows you to release emotional blockages, improve your physical and emotional health, and live in full harmony with yourself and others. The key is consistency and patience in your practice, staying attuned to signs of imbalance, and adjusting your methods accordingly to maintain a fluid and balanced energy.

To ensure the benefits of spiritual release and the opening of inner chakras endure, it is crucial to integrate regular practices into your daily life.

Incorporate meditation, conscious breathing, and affirmations into your daily routine. These practices strengthen your inner connection and support your emotional well-being.

Regularly reassess your emotional and spiritual state to identify areas needing attention or adjustment. This helps you stay aligned with your healing and growth goals.

Maintain a physical and mental space dedicated to peace and reflection. A well-maintained sacred space provides a constant refuge for your spiritual and emotional development.

Surround yourself with people who support your spiritual journey, and participating in support groups or spiritual communities can enrich your practice and offer additional perspectives.

Finally, cultivate gratitude and letting go to strengthen your resilience in facing challenges. These practices foster a positive attitude and an open mind for continuous evolution.

Chapter VIII
Finding Healing in Gratitude and Self-Love

Gratitude and self-love are essential pillars for emotional healing and personal growth. Cultivating these practices can profoundly transform our perception of ourselves and our life experience, soothing emotional wounds and fostering lasting well-being. This chapter explores how to develop a daily gratitude practice to strengthen self-love and heal wounds, with concrete examples and practical exercises to guide you on this path.

Gratitude is a powerful emotion that connects us to the present and helps us appreciate the positive aspects of our lives, even during difficult times. Cultivating gratitude can shift our mindset from one of lack to one of abundance, reducing feelings of stress, anxiety, and depression.

Gratitude is important because it changes our perspective. It helps you see the positive side of things, even when situations are challenging. By focusing on what you have rather than what you lack, you shift your perspective and foster a positive mindset.

Additionally, it strengthens relationships. By expressing gratitude, you enhance your interpersonal relationships, strengthening bonds and increasing feelings of connection and kindness.

Regular gratitude practice is associated with reduced cortisol levels, the stress hormone, and improved overall well-being. Therefore, incorporating gratitude into your daily routine can transform your life. To cultivate and make it a habit, you can keep a gratitude journal. Writing regularly is a proven method to reinforce feelings of appreciation and recognition. This exercise helps you focus on the positive aspects of your life.

To do this, set aside a moment each day, either in the morning or evening, to write in your journal and note three to five things you are grateful for each day. These can be events, people, or even small things like a beautiful sunset or a received smile. Then, describe why you are grateful for each item. This helps deepen your appreciation and connect more fully with gratitude.

Mindfulness enhances the ability to appreciate the present moment and cultivate feelings of gratitude. By practicing mindfulness alongside gratitude meditation, you focus on what is good in the present moment and the positive aspects of your life. To do this, sit comfortably in a quiet place and close your eyes. Take a few deep breaths and focus on a person, experience, or aspect of your life for which you feel gratitude. Imagine this person or situation clearly in your mind. Then, try to feel the emotions of gratitude in your heart and allow these feelings to grow and fill your entire being. Repeat gratitude affirmations such as, "I am deeply grateful for [insert object of your gratitude]."

The second phase of this exercise is to express your gratitude directly to those around you. This strengthens bonds and brings happiness to both you and those who receive your recognition.

You can also write a gratitude letter. Choose someone in your life to whom you wish to express your gratitude and start drafting a letter where you sincerely communicate what you appreciate about this person and how they have positively impacted your life. Once done, send your letter or deliver it directly to the person. You can also read it aloud during a meeting.

Self-love is essential for emotional healing. By practicing gratitude towards yourself, you can strengthen your self-esteem and develop a positive relationship with yourself. Positive affirmations are statements that boost your self-confidence and self-love. They help counteract negative thoughts and reinforce your self-image.

To create and develop positive affirmations that reflect your qualities, successes, and personal worth, repeat statements like: "I deserve love and respect," "I am proud of who I am and what I achieve," "I am worthy of happiness and success." Repeat these affirmations daily, preferably in front of a mirror, focusing on the meaning and truth of the words.

Acts of self-love involve taking concrete steps to care for yourself. This can include actions that nurture your body, mind, and soul. Practice self-love rituals by setting aside time each week to do something you love and that brings you joy, whether it's reading a book, taking a relaxing bath, or engaging in a creative activity.

Also, take time for physical self-care and engage in practices that nurture your body, such as exercising, eating healthily, or receiving a massage. Learn to set healthy boundaries by allowing yourself to say no when necessary to protect your personal space and well-being.

Self-forgiveness is crucial for healing emotional wounds and developing self-love. We often tend to be very hard on ourselves, which can hinder our healing. To release this, reflect on moments when you judged yourself harshly and felt guilty. Write down these situations in a journal. Use writing to create a letter to yourself where you express forgiveness for these mistakes, acknowledging that you acted with the best intentions at the time. Then read your letter aloud and visualize feelings of guilt and judgment dissolving, releasing all the pressure you've put on yourself.

Gratitude and self-love are powerful practices for transforming your emotional life and fostering deep healing. By developing a daily gratitude practice, you can enhance your sense of well-being and connection with the world around you. Simultaneously, by nurturing self-love, you offer yourself the compassion, respect, and understanding needed to heal emotional wounds and cultivate a fulfilling life.

These practices require consistency and patience, but the results are worthwhile. You will discover a new depth in your ability to appreciate moments in your life, to forgive yourself, and to love yourself authentically. Gratitude and self-love, as foundations of your daily practice, will create a path toward lasting healing and a harmonious life.

Chapter IX
Letting Go: Detachment and Spiritual Resilience

The art of letting go and spiritual resilience are crucial skills for navigating life's emotional challenges. Learning to detach from attachments and cultivate resilience allows you to face difficulties with increased serenity and to grow despite obstacles. This chapter explores the principles of letting go and spiritual resilience, providing practical exercises to develop these skills and overcome emotional challenges.

Letting go is a process of freeing yourself from expectations, the need for control, and attachments that hold you back and cause you suffering. It is an act of courage and wisdom that allows you to accept reality as it is and find inner peace despite external circumstances. The art of letting go is important because it plays a major role in reducing stress. Letting go decreases the pressure you put on yourself to control or change situations beyond your control, thus reducing stress and anxiety. It also frees you emotionally, allowing you to detach from negative emotions and limiting thoughts that can imprison you and prevent you from living fully. By accepting what you cannot change and focusing on what you can influence, you create opportunities for personal and spiritual growth.

To learn to let go, it is essential to accept what is. Letting go begins with accepting reality as it is, without judgment or resistance. This means recognizing and accepting your emotions and situations you cannot control. Through acceptance meditation, you can naturally and easily let go. Sit in a quiet place, close your eyes, and take a few deep breaths to center yourself. Imagine a situation or emotion you have difficulty accepting. Visualize yourself accepting this situation with compassion and without judgment, and repeat affirmations such as, "I accept what I cannot change. I find peace in accepting reality as it is."

Letting go involves relinquishing the need to control everything and releasing rigid expectations about how things should be. To release expectations and control needs, note the specific expectations you have of others and how these expectations cause you stress or disappointment. Reflect on each expectation and ask yourself if it is realistic or if it prevents you from finding peace, and write affirmations to release these expectations, such as, "I choose to let go of what I cannot control."

Detachment is not indifference but the ability to maintain emotional balance while staying connected to others and situations. Identify a relationship or situation in which you feel excessively attached or controlling and practice mindful observation by emotionally detaching from this situation. Try to view things as an impartial observer without being overwhelmed by your emotions.

Use spiritual resilience in parallel. This is the ability to bounce back from adversity, find meaning in challenges, and maintain a positive perspective despite difficulties. It is an essential quality for facing the ups and downs of life with strength and courage. It is crucial because it strengthens your inner strength. Resilience helps us draw on our inner strength to overcome challenges and trials, finding support in our spirituality and deep values.

It allows you to find meaning in difficulties and maintain a positive perspective, even when circumstances are tough. Moreover, resilience helps you adapt to changes and evolve in response to challenges, making you more flexible and open to personal growth.

To develop spiritual resilience, find meaning in challenges and seek purpose in trials to transform a difficult experience into an opportunity for growth and learning. Identify a recent difficulty you have encountered and write about how this trial has affected your life and what you have learned from this experience. Then reflect on how this experience can help you grow spiritually and write affirmations about finding meaning in challenges, such as, "Each trial is an opportunity for my personal growth."

Even in difficult times, gratitude for the lessons learned can enhance resilience and transform the way we experience trials. To acknowledge the gratitude you have gained, make a list of challenges you have faced and note one positive thing or lesson you have learned from each. Reflect on how these lessons have helped you grow and evolve. Express your gratitude for these lessons by writing a gratitude statement, such as, "I am grateful for the challenges I have faced as they have allowed me to grow."

Cultivating meditation and mindfulness strengthens resilience by helping you stay present, calm, and centered, even in times of stress. Practice resilience meditation by sitting comfortably in a quiet place. Close your eyes, focus on your breathing, and visualize yourself facing a challenge with calm and serenity. Imagine yourself finding solutions and maintaining a positive perspective while repeating affirmations like, "I am resilient in the face of challenges. I find peace and inner strength in every situation."

Subsequently, rely on a spiritual support network and surround yourself with people and communities who share your spiritual values, as they can enhance your resilience by offering support and encouragement.

Identify individuals or groups that provide spiritual and emotional support and spend time with them or participate in support groups. Share your experiences and receive encouragement and spiritual perspectives.

The art of letting go and spiritual resilience are essential skills for navigating emotional challenges and finding inner peace. By learning to accept what you cannot change, releasing rigid expectations, and developing a perspective of gratitude and meaning in trials, you can cultivate inner strength and lasting serenity. These practices require patience and practice, but they pave the way for a more harmonious and resilient life. By integrating these exercises into your daily routine, you will strengthen your ability to face challenges with a positive attitude and an open heart. Letting go and resilience are not destinations but an ongoing journey towards a more balanced and meaningful life.

Chapter X
Creating a Sacred Space to Nourish Your Soul

A sacred space is both a physical and mental environment that fosters spiritual healing and emotional well-being. By creating an environment that nourishes your soul, you establish a personal sanctuary where you can recharge, meditate, and cultivate inner peace. This chapter explores how to create a sacred space that supports your spiritual and emotional growth, and how to maintain this practice over time for lasting well-being.

Having a sacred space is particularly important because it is an environment that helps you reconnect with yourself, find tranquility, and nurture your spirit. It can serve as a refuge from daily stress, a place for meditation, prayer, or simply a spot to relax and rejuvenate. Creating a sacred space is a way to take care of yourself and strengthen your connection with your deeper essence.

Possessing a sacred space is crucial as it allows you to significantly reduce your stress levels. Indeed, a space dedicated to inner peace offers a haven where you can escape from daily chaos and lower stress. Additionally, it helps enhance your concentration as a calm and organized environment promotes focus and reflection, essential for meditation and spiritual growth. Moreover, it encourages spiritual rituals since a sacred space provides a framework for regular spiritual practices such as meditation, prayer, or journaling, reinforcing your commitment to personal development.

Creating a physical sacred space begins with selecting a spot in your home or environment where you can retreat for reflection, meditation, or other spiritual practices. Choose a quiet place where you can be free from distractions. This could be a corner of your living room, a dedicated room, or even an outdoor space. The goal is to select a place that makes you feel calm and centered. Walk through your home to identify potential spots, and choose an area that attracts you and is sufficiently removed from daily distractions. Designate this space as your sacred area and commit to keeping it free from distractions.

Once you have chosen the location, arrange the space according to your spiritual and emotional needs. Use soothing colors and natural materials to create a serene atmosphere. Soft tones like light blue, green, or neutral colors promote relaxation. Include essential elements such as a meditation cushion, a comfortable chair, or a rug, ensuring that the furniture is functional and harmonizes with the space. Feel free to add personal elements that inspire you, such as candles, crystals, plants, or spiritual objects. These elements can help create an ambiance conducive to meditation and contemplation.

To set up your space, select objects and decorations that evoke peace and serenity for you. For instance, you might add scented candles or a small altar with meaningful items. Arrange these elements in your space to create a harmonious and inviting environment. Ensure that the space remains clear and orderly to support concentration.

A sacred space should remain clean and organized to maintain an atmosphere of calm and serenity. Ensure that this space reflects your commitment to well-being by scheduling regular sessions to clean and reorganize your sacred space. Make sure the space remains free from anything that might create clutter or distractions. Periodically check if the items present continue to inspire and bring you peace. Replace or rearrange objects as needed.

You can also create a mental sacred space. This is an inner zone where you cultivate peace, clarity, and serenity. It involves developing habits and practices that promote mental tranquility and emotional well-being. Establish a regular spiritual routine that helps you maintain a calm and centered mindset. This might include practices such as meditation, journaling, or personal reflection.

To establish a routine, identify the spiritual or wellness practices you want to incorporate into your daily routine. This could be a morning meditation, affirmations, or time for reflection, and set regular times for these practices so they become an integral part of your daily routine.

Continue practicing mindfulness as it helps you stay present and manage stress and emotions more effectively. By cultivating mindfulness, you can maintain inner tranquility even outside your sacred space.

To practice mindfulness meditation, choose a meditation technique that suits you, such as mindfulness meditation or conscious breathing. Practice regularly and dedicate a few minutes each day to mindfulness. Focus on your breath, bodily sensations, or your immediate environment to cultivate a state of presence.

Emotional resilience helps you face life's challenges with calm and inner strength. Developing resilience enhances your ability to maintain a sacred mental space even during stressful periods.

Utilize resilience journaling by noting challenging situations you have faced and how you overcame them. Identify strategies that helped you stay resilient and consider techniques for strengthening your emotional resilience, such as social support, practicing gratitude, or finding meaning in challenges.

Creating a sacred space is a long-term commitment that requires ongoing effort to maintain its effectiveness. To ensure the longevity of your sacred space, both physical and mental, regularly reassess its effectiveness and adjust it according to your changing needs. A sacred space should evolve with you to continue supporting your spiritual growth.

Periodically evaluate the effectiveness of your sacred space by scheduling regular check-ins, such as once a month or each season. Reflect on what is working well and what could be improved, and make the necessary adjustments to maintain its effectiveness. Maintaining a consistent practice in your sacred space is essential to fully reap its benefits. Commit to using this space regularly for your spiritual and emotional practices by creating a practice schedule where you can plan your sessions. Create a calendar for your spiritual and emotional activities in your sacred space. Include times for meditation, journaling, and other practices. Ensure you adhere to this schedule and commit to following it to ensure you are regularly using your sacred space.

Creating and maintaining a sacred space is a crucial step in nourishing your soul and promoting emotional well-being. By designing a physical and mental space that fosters tranquility, focus, and spiritual growth, you provide yourself with a valuable refuge for healing and personal development. This process requires ongoing commitment and regular attention to maintain the effectiveness of your sacred space. By integrating these practices into your daily life and regularly reassessing your needs, you will create a lasting sanctuary that supports your emotional and spiritual well-being.

Ultimately, a sacred space is more than just a place; it is a manifestation of your commitment to yourself and your growth. By caring for this space, you invest in your own inner peace and spiritual development, thus laying a solid foundation for a fulfilling and balanced life.

Conclusion
Spiritual Liberation and the Opening of Inner Chakras

Through the chapters of this guide, you have embarked on a profound journey toward spiritual healing and emotional well-being, focusing on essential practices and tools to unlock your inner potential and harmonize your existence. This journey, which includes embracing pain, mindfulness, conscious breathing, forgiveness, intention, connecting with your inner child, chakra balancing, gratitude, letting go, and creating a sacred space, offers significant benefits for your personal and spiritual development. This conclusion summarizes these concepts and highlights the importance of spiritual liberation and the opening of inner chakras in your path toward deep and lasting balance.

Spiritual liberation is an essential process for freeing yourself from emotional chains and mental blockages that prevent you from living fully. It involves reconnecting with your deep essence, accepting past wounds, and transforming your state of being. This journey begins with embracing pain and opening to mindfulness, which allows you to understand and process difficult emotions with a broader and more serene perspective.

By embracing pain, you pave the way for authentic healing. Understanding and accepting your emotional wounds with compassion initiates the healing process that enables you to release the burdens of the past. Mindfulness helps you stay present in the moment, observe your thoughts and emotions without judgment, and cultivate an inner space of peace and clarity.

Conscious breathing is a powerful technique for unraveling tension and releasing blocked energies. By using targeted breathing practices, you can achieve a state of deep relaxation, which allows you to dissolve emotional blockages and promote a smooth flow of energy throughout your being.

Forgiveness, both toward yourself and others, plays a crucial role in spiritual liberation. It allows you to release resentments and negative feelings that hold you back, offering a path to healing and reconciliation.

Forgiveness is not only an act of mercy but also a means to free your own heart and regain inner peace.

Intention is a powerful tool for transforming your inner reality. By using positive affirmations and clear intentions, you reprogram your mind and direct your energy toward healing and growth goals. This practice enables you to overcome limiting beliefs and heal negative emotions, creating a space conducive to personal flourishing.

Reconnecting with your inner child is an essential step toward regaining inner harmony. Childhood emotional wounds can have a profound impact on your adult life. By reintegrating your inner child with love and compassion, you heal these wounds and restore emotional balance, allowing you to live more authentically and joyfully.

Chakra balancing plays a fundamental role in harmonizing your emotional body. Each chakra, or energy center, is linked to specific aspects of your emotional and spiritual well-being. By working on opening and balancing these chakras, you promote a harmonious flow of energy, contributing to an overall state of health and serenity. The opening and balancing of inner chakras offer a multitude of benefits for your overall well-being. Each chakra plays a specific role in our emotional and spiritual development. To ensure the lasting benefits of spiritual liberation and the opening of inner chakras, it is crucial to integrate regular practices into our daily lives.

In conclusion, spiritual liberation and the opening of inner chakras are essential aspects of your journey toward well-being and personal fulfillment. By incorporating these practices into your daily life and committing to a continuous process of growth and healing, you create a harmonious inner space that allows you to live with profound serenity, enhanced clarity, and an authentic connection with your spiritual essence.

"May your journey toward healing and self-discovery be rich and transformative, bringing lasting balance and deep joy into every aspect of your life."

Printed in Great Britain
by Amazon